Epics for Students, Second Edition, Volume 2

Project Editor: Sara Constantakis Rights Acquisition and Management: Margaret Chamberlain-Gaston, Savannah Gignac, Tracie Richardson, Jhanay Williams Composition: Evi Abou-El-Seoud

Manufacturing: Drew Kalasky

Imaging: John Watkins

Product Design: Pamela A. E. Galbreath, Jennifer Wahi Content Conversion: Katrina Coach Product Manager: Meggin Condino

ISBN-13: 978-1-4144-7621-6 (set)
ISBN-13: 978-1-4144-7622-3 (vol. 1)
ISBN-13: 978-1-4144-7623-0 (vol. 2) ISBN-10: 1-4144-7621-3 (set)
ISBN-10: 1-4144-7622-1 (vol. 1)
ISBN-10: 1-4144-7623-X (vol. 2) This title is also available as an e-book.
ISBN-13: 978-1-4144-7624-7
ISBN-10: 1-4144-7624-8
Contact your Gale, a part of Cengage Learning sales representative for ordering information.

Printed in the United States of America
1 2 3 4 5 6 7 14 13 12 11 10

Odyssey

Homer

C. 700 BCE

Introduction

Homer's *Odyssey* is generally considered to be the sequel to the *Iliad*. Unlike many sequels in the modern era, however, the *Odyssey* actually seems to be an improvement, in some respects, on the original and is quite capable of standing as an independent work.

Odysseia, which has been this poem's name in Greek since Herodotus called it that in the fifth century BCE, means simply "the story of Odysseus." That story refers to the ten-year-long return trip of

Odysseus from Troy to his island home of Ithaca, off the west coast of Greece. Because the epic pertains to this long journey, the term *odyssey* has since come to mean any significant and difficult journey.

For more than fifteen hundred years, the *Iliad* and the *Odyssey* set the western standard by which epic poetry was judged. The epic form in poetry seemed to die out with Milton's *Paradise Lost*, but the story of Odysseus has remained a perennial favorite. Robert Fagles's translation of the *Odyssey*, a Penguin Classics edition, appeared in 2006.

Author Biography

Everything known about Homer is either traditional, mythical, or some kind of an educated guess. Traditionally, probably following the *Odyssey* and one of the so-called Homeric hymns from the middle of the seventh century BCE, Homer, like his own character Demodocus, was believed to be a blind bard or singer of tales.

At least seven different places have claimed that Homer was born on their soil in the ancient world. The two with the strongest claims are the island of Chios and the city of Smyrna (modern Izmir, in Turkey). Because he records many details of Ionian geography and seems to know less about other areas (like western Greece, where part of the *Odyssey* is set), and because the most common dialect in Homer's Greek is Ionic, many scholars believe that Homer probably lived and worked in Ionia, the region along the west coast of what is now Turkey.

When Homer lived and wrote is open for debate. Some ancient writers believed that Homer lived relatively close to the time of the events he described. The fifth-century historian Herodotus in his *Histories* said that Homer could not possibly have lived more than four hundred years before the fifth century. Nonetheless, the rediscovery of writing by the Greeks around 750 BCE and the development, at about the same time, of some of the fighting techniques described in the *Iliad* have led scholars to assign Homer to the middle or late part of the eighth century BCE

Accurate dating of Homer's poems is impossible, but it is generally thought that the *Iliad* is the older of the two, as the *Odyssey* displays certain advanced stylistic features. Both poems were completed before the Peisistratid dynasty came to power in Athens in the sixth century BCE, as a member of that family commissioned a standard edition of the poems and ordered that both the *Iliad* and the *Odyssey* be recited in full at the Great Panathenaia, a religious festival in honor of Athena, which was observed in Athens every four years.

There have been various controversies about Homer since his time, beginning with the contention over just exactly where and when he was born, lived, and died. Some scholars have questioned whether Homer existed at all, whether he actually wrote the poems attributed to him or compiled them from popular folklore, and whether the same person is responsible for both the *Iliad* and the *Odyssey*.

Many scholars likely would agree that there was an epic poet called Homer and that this poet was instrumental in producing the *Iliad* and *Odyssey* in their known forms.

The Background to the Story

After ten years, the Trojan War is over and the Achaeans head for home, with varying results. Some, like Nestor, come home quickly to find things pretty much as they left them. Others, like Agamemnon, make it home quickly but find things considerably changed. Still others, like Menelaus, wander for a time but eventually return home safely and little the worse for wear.

Odysseus, by contrast, has no end of trouble getting home. As the story opens, it is the tenth year since the end of the war, a full twenty years since Odysseus sailed off for Troy with the rest of the Achaean forces.

Book 1: Athena Inspires Telemachus

In a council of the gods, Athena asks her father why Odysseus is still stuck on Calypso's island, ten years after the end of the war. Zeus responds that Poseidon is angry at Odysseus for having blinded his son, Polyphemus. But since Poseidon is temporarily out of the country, so to speak, Zeus gives her permission to begin arrangements for Odysseus's return. Athena goes to Ithaca in disguise and inspires Odysseus's son Telemachus to go in search of news of his father. Heartened by her words, Telemachus announces his intention to sail to the mainland.

Media Adaptations

- In 1641, Claudio Monteverdi composed the opera *Il Ritorno d'Ulisse in Patria* (*The Return of Ulysses*), treating Odysseus's return to Ithaca after his journey.

- In 1928, Richard Strauss composed the opera *Die a gyptische Helena*, based on the account of Helen's visit to Egypt in Book 4 of the *Odyssey*.

- In 1954, Dino De Laurentiis produced the film *Ulisse* (released in English as *Ulysses* in the same year), directed by Mario Camerini and starring Kirk Douglas as Ulysses and Anthony Quinn as Antinoos. This film was re-released as a DVD in 2009.

- In 1963, Pietro Francisci directed the film *Ercole sfida Sansone*, released in 1965 in the United States as *Hercules, Samson, and Ulysses*.

- The 1967 British film *Ulysses*, based on the 1922 James Joyce novel by the same title, starred Martin Dempsey and Barbara Jefford.

- In 1967, the British rock band Cream, made up of Eric Clapton, Jack Bruce, and Ginger Baker, recorded the song "Tales of Brave Ulysses" on their second album, *Disraeli Gears*. The song includes characters, themes, and motifs from the epic.

- There is at least a symbolic link between Homer's poem and the classic 1968 MGM production *2001: A Space Odyssey*, directed by Stanley Kubrick and starring Keir Dullea.

- In 1969, Radiotelevisione Italiana (RAI) produced a television version of the epic, directed by Mario Bara and Franco Rossi.

- In May 1997, NBC television produced a two-part miniseries of the *Odyssey*, starring Armand Assante, Isabella Rossellini, Vanessa Williams, and Irene Pappas. This production was re-released on DVD by Lions gate Studios in 2001.

- The 1996 Penguin High bridge Audio cassette of the *Odyssey* uses the Robert Fagles translation and is narrated by Sir Ian McKellen.

- The 2000 Universal Pictures film *O Brother, Where Art Thou?* is a comical remake of the *Odyssey* set in the 1930s South with bluegrass music.

- Noted storyteller Sebastian Lockwood produced a one-man video of his performance of the *Odyssey* in 2006.

- The Perseus Project at Tufts University, which was available as of 2010 on CD-ROM from Yale University Press, offers both the original Greek text and the Loeb Classical Library translation in English, together with background information on many of the characters and places in the poem.

Book 2: Telemachus Sails to Pylos

Telemachus calls an assembly and asks for assistance in getting to the mainland. His independent attitude does not sit well with his mother's suitors, who oppose him in the assembly so that he does not receive the aid he seeks. After making secret preparations, Telemachus and the disguised Athena depart for Pylos that same evening.

Book 3: Nestor Tells What He Knows

Telemachus and Athena arrive in Pylos to find Nestor and his family offering sacrifice to Poseidon. After joining in the ritual, Telemachus introduces himself to Nestor and explains his purpose in coming. Nestor has heard news of the return of both Menelaus and Agamemnon, which he relates to Telemachus, but has had no news of Odysseus since sailing home from Troy ten years previously. Nestor sends Telemachus, accompanied by one of his sons, Pisistratus, to visit Menelaus in Sparta.

Book 4: In the Home of Menelaus and Helen

Telemachus and Pisistratus arrive at Menelaus's home as he is celebrating awedding and are warmly entertained by Menelaus and Helen. Menelaus tells a long story of his adventures on the way home from Troy, including news that he got from Proteus in Egypt that Odysseus was alive on Calypso's island. Meanwhile, back in Ithaca, the suitors learn of Telemachus's secret departure and are not pleased. They plot to ambush and kill him on his way home. Penelope also learns of her son's departure.

Book 5: Odysseus Sets Sail for Home and Gets Shipwrecked

At another council of the gods, Zeus orders Hermes to go to Calypso and tell her that she is to let Odysseus leave for Ithaca. Calypso is unhappy, but obeys the order. She offers Odysseus a chance to become immortal and to live with her forever, an offer which he tactfully declines. Odysseus builds a raft with tools and materials she provides and sails toward home until Poseidon comes back from feasting with the Ethiopians and wrecks the raft in a storm. Odysseus, with the help of a sea goddess, is washed safely ashore in the land of the Phaeacians.

Book 6: Nausicaa Encounters a Stranger

Inspired in a dream by Athena, the Princess Nausicaa goes with several of her maids to do the royal laundry. The washing place is near where Odysseus has fallen asleep, hidden in a bush. Odysseus asks Nausicaa for help; she gives him some clothing to wear and sends him into town to find the palace of her father, Alcinous.

Book 7: Odysseus and the King of Phaeacia

Odysseus arrives safely at the palace and begs the assistance of King Alcinous and Queen Arete. He gives an edited version of his adventures to date but does not disclose his identity. He deftly turns aside Alcinous's suggestion that he should remain in Phaeacia and marry Nausicaa.

Book 8: The Phaeacians Entertain Odysseus

The Phaeacians treat Odysseus to a day of feasting, song, and athletic events. When Odysseus begins weeping during Demodocus's tale of the Trojan War, Alcinous cuts the banquet short. At dinner that evening, Odysseus speaks highly of Demodocus's skill and offers him a prime cut of his own portion. When Demodocus sings the story of the Trojan Horse, Odysseus begins crying again, and Alcinous asks Odysseus who he is and why stories about Troy make him cry.

Book 9: Odysseus Tells His Story— Polyphemus and the Cyclopes

Odysseus reveals his identity and tells his story, beginning with his departure from Troy with twelve ships. He sacks Ismarus in Thrace, is blown off course to the land of the Lotus-Eaters, and eventually reaches the island of the Cyclopes, one-eyed giants who live in rustic anarchy.

Odysseus and the crew of his ship go to investigate this island and end up in Polyphemus's cave. The giant rolls a stone across the cave's entrance, and, finding strangers inside, promptly turns a couple of Odysseus's men into his dinner. After a similar breakfast, he goes out with his flocks, leaving Odysseus and his men penned in the cave. Upon Polyphemus's return, they manage to get the giant drunk, blind him, and then sneak out of the cave under the bellies of his sheep and goats. As they make their escape, Odysseus unwisely reveals his true name, and Polyphemus asks his father Poseidon to avenge his injury.

Book 10: Odysseus Tells His Story —At the Islands of Aeolus and Circe

Odysseus and his surviving crewmen now sail to the island of Aeolus, king of the winds. Aeolus gives Odysseus a bag containing all the winds that would prevent his reaching home. They sail away and come close enough to Ithaca to see the watch-fires, when Odysseus falls asleep at the helm and his crew, thinking the bag contains a hoard of gold, untie it and release the captive winds, which blow them right back to Aeolus's island.

Aeolus refuses to have anything more to do with them. Odysseus and his crew set sail once more and eventually reach the land of the

Laestrygonians, who destroy all but one of his ships. The survivors sail to Circe's island, where most of them are promptly turned into pigs. Odysseus, forewarned by Hermes, avoids the sorceress's trap and frees his men. They remain with Circe for a year before Odysseus's men ask to leave. Circe tells Odysseus that he must first visit the underworld and consult with the shade of the prophet Tiresias on how best to get home.

Book 11: Odysseus Tells His Story —In the House of the Dead

Obeying Circe's instructions, Odysseus and his men sail to the underworld where they make sacrifices to Hades and Persephone and consult Tiresias. When Tiresias retires, the shades of Odysseus's mother and several of his comrades at Troy appear, including those of Achilles and Agamemnon. Odysseus also witnesses the punishment of several notorious offenders against the gods.

Book 12: Odysseus Tells His Story —The Sun-God's Cattle

Upon his return from the underworld, Odysseus receives sailing instructions from Circe on how to avoid the lure of the Sirens and how to get past the monster Scylla and the whirlpool Charybdis. Above all, Circe warns Odysseus not to harm the cattle of the sun-god on the island of Thrinacia. Cast upon Thrinacia by a fierce storm and out of provisions,

Odysseus's men disobey him and slaughter some of the cattle. The sun-god complains to Zeus, who destroys the ship with a thunderbolt. Only Odysseus survives, and he drifts to Calypso's island by hanging on to the ship's mast. This ends Odysseus's story as told to the Phaeacians.

Book 13: Return to Ithaca and the Stone Ship

The Phaeacians land Odysseus and all his treasures on Ithaca while he himself is deep asleep. Athena, in disguise, meets Odysseus, and he tries to trick her, without success, with a false story about himself. She reveals her identity and tells him how much she cares for him, and they plot a stratagem for dealing with Penelope's suitors. After stowing Odysseus's treasure safely in a cave, Athena disguises Odysseus as an ancient beggar and sends him on his way. Poseidon, angry that the Phaeacians have helped Odysseus get back to Ithaca, turns their ship into a huge stone, visible to onlookers on shore and rooted to the sea-bottom, as it sails into harbor on its return voyage.

Book 14: The Loyal Swineherd

Odysseus makes his way to the dwelling of Eumaeus, a swineherd who has remained loyal to his long-absent employer. Odysseus, still in disguise, entertains Eumaeus with some "lying tales" about himself.

Book 15: Telemachus Heads for Home

Telemachus takes his leave of Helen and Menelaus and tactfully evades Nestor's further hospitality.

Telemachus offers passage to the seer Theoclymenus, who is fleeing vengeance for a kinsman's death. Back in Ithaca, Eumaeus tells Odysseus the story of his life. Telemachus evades the suitors' ambush and sends Theoclymenus home with a friend, as he intends to visit Eumaeus in the country before returning to the palace and the suitors.

Book 16: Father and Son Reunited

Telemachus goes to Eumaeus's hut, where Odysseus reveals himself to his son and impresses on him the need for secrecy and deception if they are to overcome the suitors. Meanwhile, the ship the suitors had sent out to ambush Telemachus returns, and the suitors try without success to come up with an alternative plan to get rid of him.

Book 17: A Beggar at the Gate

Telemachus returns to the palace and speaks with his mother. Eumaeus brings Odysseus to the palace. On the way they encounter the goatherd Melanthius, an ally of the suitors, who insults Odysseus. As Odysseus enters the palace, an old hunting dog recognizes him and dies on the spot. Most of the suitors treat Odysseus with at least grudging respect, but Antinous throws a footstool at him. Penelope asks Eumaeus to arrange a meeting with the new visitor.

Book 18: The Two Beggar-Kings

Odysseus is insulted by Irus, a professional beggar whom the suitors favor. The two men fight, much to the amusement of the suitors, and Odysseus quickly subdues Irus. Penelope comes to the hall to extract presents from the suitors and to announce her intention of remarrying. Odysseus is insulted by the maid Melantho and Eurymachus, one of the leading suitors, who throws another footstool at him.

Book 19: Penelope Interrogates Her Guest

Odysseus and his son take all the weapons from the great hall, assisted by Athena. Melantho again insults Odysseus. Penelope speaks to the beggar, who claims to know Odysseus and tells her that he is nearby and will be home quickly. She does not believe him but orders his old nurse, Eurycleia, to wash him. The nurse recognizes Odysseus by a scar he received as a young man and is sworn to secrecy. Penelope details the trial of the bow by which she will choose her new husband on the following day.

Book 20: Things Begin to Look

Bad for the Suitors

Odysseus lays awake plotting revenge until Athena puts him to sleep. On the next day, the loyal ox herd Philoetius arrives at the palace, where Odysseus is again insulted by one of the suitors, Ctesippus, who throws an ox-foot at him. The suitors all laugh at this, which Theoclymenus interprets as a sign that they are all marked for death.

Book 21: The Great Bow of Odysseus

Penelope fetches Odysseus's hunting bow and announces the test: She will marry the man who can string the bow and shoot an arrow through the rings on twelve axe-heads set in a line in the ground. Odysseus reveals himself to his two loyal servants and enlists their help in getting revenge on the suitors. None of the suitors is able to string the bow; Telemachus is on the point of succeeding when Odysseus stops him. Telemachus, by prearrangement with his father, sends his mother from the hall and gives the bow to Odysseus, who strings it and shoots an arrow through the axes.

Book 22: The Death of the Suitors

With his next arrow, Odysseus shoots Antinous and announces his true identity to the rest of the suitors. Odysseus, Telemachus, Philoetius, and Eumaeus, assisted by the disguised Athena, kill the suitors. When all the suitors are dead, the disloyal maids are hanged, and Melanthius is punished. The loyal servants begin to clean the palace after the slaughter.

Book 23: The Reunion

Old Eurycleia wakes Penelope with the news that her husband has returned and destroyed the suitors. Penelope refuses to believe it. When Odysseus answers her trick question about their marriage bed, she accepts him as her husband, and they retire to bed after making plans to deal with the relatives of the suitors whom Odysseus has just killed. Before they sleep, Odysseus tells his wife his true story.

Book 24: Peace at Last

The suitors' shades arrive in Hades and tell Agamemnon and Achilles of Odysseus's triumphant revenge on them for their destruction of his estate. Odysseus goes to meet his aged father Laertes in the country and, after telling him another "lying tale," reveals himself to his father. The suitors' relatives arrive at that point, seeking vengeance for the death of their kinsmen. Athena and Zeus intervene in the fighting that ensues and, after a few of the suitors' relatives are killed, Athena makes peace.

Achilles

Son of the mortal Peleus and the sea goddess Thetis, Achilles was the best warrior at the siege of Troy. Odysseus encounters his shade (spirit) in the underworld in Book 11 while waiting for the seer Tiresias to tell him how he is to return home after being delayed for ten years.

Achilleus

See Achilles

Aeacides

See Achilles

Aeolus

The son of Hippotas, Aeolus is beloved of the gods and Zeus put him in charge of the winds. He and his family (six sons married to six daughters) live on Aeolia, a floating island. After listening to Odysseus's tales of Troy, he agrees to help and makes Odysseus a present of a bag containing all the adverse winds that could blow him off his proper course home. Unfortunately, Odysseus's men untie the knot, thinking they will find gold in the bag, and the winds blow them back to Aeolia. Aeolus casts them out, saying he has no desire to help anyone who is so obviously cursed by the gods.

Agamemnon

Son of Atreus, brother of Menelaus, and king of Mycenae, Agamemnon was the commander of the Achaean forces at Troy. Odysseus encounters his shade in the underworld while waiting for the seer Tiresias to tell him how to get home after ten years of wandering.

Aias

See Ajax

Ajax (Oilean, the Lesser)

Son of Oileus and leader of the Locrians at Troy, Ajax is shipwrecked on his way home after the war. He boasts of having escaped the sea in spite of the gods—and is subsequently drowned by Poseidon. Odysseus encounters his shade in the underworld in Book 11.

Ajax (Telamonian, the Greater

Son of Telamon and grandson of Aeacus (who was also grandfather of Achilles), Ajax was one of the bravest and strongest fighters at Troy. Odysseus encounters the shade of Ajax in the underworld and apologizes for the outcome of their contest at Achilles's funeral games, but Ajax, angry with Odysseus even after death, refuses to speak to the man he believes had unfairly beaten him in life.

Ajax the Greater

See Ajax (Telamonian, the Greater)

Ajax the Lesser

See Ajax (Oilean, the Lesser)

Akhilleus

See Achilles

Alcinous

Son of Nausithous, husband of Arete, and father of Nausicaa and Laodamas, Alcinous, whose name means *sharp-witted* or *brave-witted*, is king of Phaeacia and a grandson of Poseidon. Homer depicts him as a kind, generous, and noble man, eager to help the stranger and put him at ease. He suggests that Odysseus should stay in Phaeacia and marry his daughter.

Antinoos

See Antinous

Antinous

Son of Eupithes, Antinous (whose name literally means *anti-mind* and could be translated as *mindless*) is a bold, ambitious, and obnoxious suitor for Penelope's hand.

Aphrodite

Aphrodite is the Greek goddess of love. According to Homer, she is the daughter of Zeus and Dione. She is married, though not faithful, to Hephaestus, god of fire and smith craft.

Apollo

The son of Zeus and Leto, and twin brother of Artemis, Apollo is the god of archery, prophecy, music, medicine, light, and youth. As is frequently seen in the *Odyssey*, plagues and other diseases, and sometimes a peaceful death in old age are often explained as being the result of "gentle arrows" shot by Apollo (for men) or by his sister Artemis (for women).

Arete

Niece and wife of Alcinous and mother of Nausicaa, Arete is queen of the Phaeacians. Her name means *virtue* or *excellence* in Greek.

Artemis

Daughter of Zeus and Leto, twin sister of Apollo, Artemis is a virgin goddess of the hunt, the moon, and, in some traditions, of childbirth and the young. As is frequently seen in the *Odyssey*, plagues and other diseases, and sometimes a peaceful death in old age, are often explained as being the result of "gentle arrows" shot by Artemis (for women) or by her brother Apollo (for men).

Athena

Athena is the daughter Metis, who Zeus (following in the tradition of his own father, Cronus) swallowed when it was revealed that she would someday bear a son who would be lord of heaven (and thus usurp Zeus's place). She was born, fully grown and in armor, from the head of Zeus after Hephaestus (or, in some traditions, Prometheus) split it open with an axe.

Athene

See Athena

Atreides

See Agamemnon

Atrides

See Agamemnon

Briseis

Briseis is the war prize given to Achilles after his attack on Lyrnessus during the Trojan War. When Agamemnon has to give up Chryseis, he takes Briseis as compensation, and this action instigates the quarrel between him and Achilles.

Calypso

Daughter of Atlas, who holds the world upon his shoulders, Calypso (whose name is related to the Greek verb *to hide* and which might therefore be translated as *concealer*) is a goddess who lives on the island of Ogygia. She has fallen in love with Odysseus during the seven years he has lived on her island and proposes to make him immortal, not a gift given lightly.

Circe

Daughter of Helios (the sun-god) and Perse, and sister of Aeetes, the king of Colchis who so plagued Jason and the Argonauts, Circe is a minor goddess who "speaks with the speech of mortals." She is also a powerful enchantress. Her specialty lies in turning men into pigs. Yet once she recognizes Odysseus and swears an oath not to harm him, she becomes the most charming of hostesses, so much so that Odysseus and his men remain with her an entire year.

Ctesippus

Ctesippus is one of the suitors for Penelope. His name literally means *horse-getter,* so he may literally be a horse-thief.

Demodocus

The blind bard, or poet, of the Phaeacian court, traditionally, Demodocus has been taken as representing Homer, but not all scholars accept this idea.

Demodokos

See Demodocus

Eumaeus

Son of Ctesius, who was king of two cities on the island of Syria (not to be confused with the Middle Eastern country of the same name), Eumaeus was kidnapped at a young age by one of his father's serving women and taken by Phoenician traders, who sold him to Laertes, Odysseus's father. Odysseus's mother, Anticleia, raised him together with her own daughter, and then sent him to the country when the daughter was married. His name might mean something like *one who seeks the good.*

Eumaios

See Eumaeus

Eurycleia

Eurycleia is the longtime servant of Odysseus's family. Odysseus's father Laertes bought her in her youth for twenty oxen, a significant price. She was Odysseus's nurse and later the nurse of Telemachus. In her old age, she attends Penelope.

Eurylochos

See Eurylochus

Eurylochus

A companion of Odysseus, Eurylochus is the one who ties Odysseus to the mast to keep him from responding—fatally—to the song of the Sirens, and it is he who leads the first group of men to Circe's palace, then has to report that they have not come back out and begs Odysseus not to make him go back. Eurylochus eventually turns on Odysseus and refuses to obey him on Thrinacia, instead urging the rest of the men to slaughter the sun-god's cattle.

Eurylokhos

See Eurylochus

Eurymachos

See Eurymachus

Eurymachus

Son of Polybus, Eurymachus is described as the "leading candidate" for Penelope's hand. His name means *wide-fighting*.

Eurymachus is arrogant, disrespectful, hypocritical, cowardly, and abusive. He is the second of the suitors to die by Odysseus's hand. Odysseus's words to him, after Eurymachus offers to make good on the damages the suitors have done to his household in his absence, are virtually the same as Achilles's words in response to Agamemnon's offer of a ransom for Briseis in Book 9 of the *Iliad*.

Eurymakhos

See Eurymachus

Helen

The wife of Menelaus, Helen went, apparently willingly, with Paris to Troy. The resulting war formed the background for Homer's other epic poem, the *Iliad*.

One might have expected Menelaus to be angry with Helen for running off to Troy, and she with him for having dragged her back. Instead, Homer describes in them a couple enjoying marital bliss: Helen and Menelaus are to all appearances deeply in love with one another and quite happy to be back in Sparta among their people and their possessions.

Kalypso

See Calypso

Kirke

See Circe

Ktesippos

See Ctesippus

Laertes

Son of Arcesius (and thus a grandson of Zeus), husband of Anticleia, and father of Odysseus, Laertes was one of those (along with Menoetius, father of Patroclus; Peleus, father of Achilles; and Telamon, father of Ajax the Greater) who sailed with Jason on the *Argo* in the quest for the Golden Fleece, according to pseudo-Apollodorus.

By the time the *Odyssey* begins, however, Laertes is old and worn by care and grief. His wife has died, his son has been absent for twenty years, first at the Trojan War and then on his wanderings home from it. Laertes has retired to a country estate, where he lives more like one of the servants than the owner.

Melanthios

See Melanthius

Melanthius

Son of Dolius, Melanthius is Odysseus's goatherd. During his master's long absence, Melanthius has become friendly with the suitors of Odysseus's wife Penelope. He insults Odysseus as Eumaeus is bringing him into town and again on the morning of the day that Odysseus kills the suitors. He attempts to bring armor from the storeroom for the suitors once Odysseus has revealed himself but is caught in the act by Eumaeus and imprisoned there until the end of the fighting. He is severely mutilated (and presumably dies of his wounds) by Telemachus, Eumaeus, and Philoetius.

Melantho

Melantho is the disloyal servant in the royal house at Ithaca. She is verbally abusive to Odysseus when he is disguised as a beggar, and she becomes the lover of one of the suitors.

Menelaus

Son of Atreus and brother of Agamemnon, Menelaus is king of Sparta and the husband of Helen. In the *Odyssey*, he shines as an example of the happy husband and father, the good ruler, and the perfect host.

Nausicaa

Daughter of Alcinous and Arete, Nausicaa is a Phaeacian princess. The night before Odysseus is discovered in the bushes, she dreams of her marriage. After Athena makes Odysseus look more regal, Nausicaa seems to think that he would make a suitable husband, a sentiment her father echoes. Her name, as with many of the Phaeacian characters, is related to the Greek word for ship, *naus*.

Nausikaa

See Nausicaa

Nestor

The only surviving son of Neleus, Nestor is the elderly king of Pylos, where it is said that he has reigned for three generations. Nestor's role is that of the elder statesman and advisor.

Odysseus

Odysseus is the son of Laertes and Anticleia, husband of Penelope, father of Telemachus, and absent king of Ithaca. This epic chronicles his ten-year journey home to Ithaca from Troy. Odysseus is a loyal husband, loving father, and a true hero who wants nothing more than to return to his home and his loved ones. To achieve this goal, he even turns down an easy chance at immortality.

Oilean

See Ajax (Oilean, the Lesser)

Pelides

See Achilles

Penelope

Penelope is the daughter of Icarius, wife of Odysseus, and mother of Telemachus. Fidelity to her husband, devotion to her son, care for the household, and resourcefulness on a par with Odysseus's own, these are the characteristics of Homer's Penelope. She is a realist; she knows there is almost no hope that Odysseus will come back after an absence of twenty years, but she will not deny that last bit of hope its chance, which sets her apart from the suitors and the faithless servants. Her test of Odysseus's identity by mentioning their marriage bed proves that she is the equal of the master of schemes himself.

Philoetius

A longtime servant of Odysseus, Philoetius manages the herds for the household. He remains loyal to his absent master; he hopes Odysseus will return but thinks it unlikely.

Philoitios

See Philoetius

Polyphemos

See Polyphemus

Polyphemus

Ason of Poseidon and one of the Cyclopes, a race of one-eyed giants living on an island which is usually thought to be Sicily, Polyphemus is presented as amember of a lawless race that does not acknowledge the gods, but who also lives in an area that provides for all their needs without effort on their part.

Poseidon

Son of Cronus and Rhea, and brother of Zeus and Hades, Poseidon is the god of the seas, earthquakes, and horses. Poseidon is stubborn and prone to holding a grudge, but not entirely unreasonable.

Teiresias

See Tiresias

Telamonian

See Ajax (Telamonian, the Greater)

Telemachos

See Telemachus

Telemachus

Son of Odysseus and Penelope, Telemachus is still a baby when Odysseus leaves for Troy. He is now grown to manhood, and his home island is beset by civil disorder and his family household besieged by men who do not want him to assume the throne. Telemachus is rather shy and diffident. He has no memories of his resourceful father to use as a model and no strong male figure to look up to or to show him the ways of a ruler.

Tiresias

Tiresias is a famous prophet from the Greek city of Thebes, the son of Everes and the nymph Chariclo. Tiresias is the only person in the underworld who has any current knowledge about the world above: Everyone else knows only what has happened up to the time of his death, unless news can be obtained from a new arrival.

Tritogeneia

See Athena

Zeus

Son of Cronus and Rhea, brother and husband of Hera, brother of Poseidon and Hades, Zeus is god of the sky and clouds, of storms and thunder, and the ruler of the other gods.

Creative and Self-protective Deception

It could be said that creativity or imagination is Odysseus's strongest trait. He is not mentioned by name for the first twenty lines of the poem, but a description appears at the end of the very first line of the poem in the word *polutropon*, which literally means *of many twists*. In modern usage, this word might be interpreted as *shifty*, except that Homer does not appear to mean anything negative by the word, merely descriptive—Odysseus is rather devious, but he has to be in order to survive.

It should be no surprise, then, to discover that Odysseus is beloved of Athena, who is the goddess of creativity and imagination. She and Odysseus have much in common, as she remarks in Book 13 (XIII.296-99), including a joy in "weaving schemes" (XIII.386).

A large part of Odysseus's creative energy is channeled into the weaving of deceptions for the people around him. In fact, Athena gives Odysseus what is either a left-handed compliment or a mild reproach in Book 13 when she says: "Wily-minded wretch, never weary of tricks, you wouldn't even dream, not even in your own native land, of giving up your wily ways, or the telling of the clever tales that are dear to you from the very root of your being" (XIII.293-95). Yet it is important to remember that Odysseus only tells such clever or *thieving* (the word can have both meanings) tales because he must; he waits until he is certain of their motives to tell the Phaeacians his true identity, but he does so when pressed. Only when he must remain anonymous to stay alive or to further some ultimate purpose does he continue a deception beyond the first moment when it could be dropped.

Heroism

Odysseus is a legitimate hero. His reputation from the *Iliad*, as recounted in the *Odyssey*, would be enough to establish that quite apart from the close relationship he has with Athena and, to a lesser degree, with Hermes. The gods only help those who are worthy; after all, none of the gods lifts a finger to help the suitors who are only getting what they deserve.

Topics for Further Study

- In a speech to his wife in Book 19, Odysseus as the beggar tells Penelope that "Odysseus would have been home long ago, but he felt in his spirit that it would be better to go all about the world collecting possessions" (282–84). The Greek word *chremata* in line 284 can be translated as *possessions* or it can mean *money* or other *valuables*, but its literal meaning is *things that are useful or needful*. What sorts of useful or needful things does Odysseus collect on his wanderings? Assign pairs of students to sections of the poem to examine the text for things Odysseus collected. Make a list on the board. Consider carefully Odysseus's character as portrayed by Homer. Do you think he was motivated by greed, necessity, or opportunity?

- Search online for a definition of *hero*. Match a definition to a story about hero in sports, in the military, in the role of first responder, or as an ordinary citizen responding in an unusual or dangerous incident. Prepare a written report with the definition, the story (with picture if available), and a paragraph of comparison to the values of Odysseus. What sorts of differences do you find, and which set of values fits your personal definition of a hero? Include your answers in your essay.

- What role do the gods play in the *Odyssey* ? Compare and contrast this role with the role of the divine in a contemporary religious tradition (your own religion or another that interests you). Share your insights in a class discussion or in an essay.

- Do an online search on the term *cultural hospitality* and compare in a written report the concept of hospitality of one or two other cultures to that of the Greeks in this epic.

- Put together a PowerPoint presentation in which you explain to your classmates the circuitous homeward route taken by Odysseus. Use art images and current and ancient maps to help your classmates visualize the journey. You might consider including information about how this trip might be taken in modern times, for example, by airplane or ship, and show current images of ports and airports in the identifiable places Odysseus reaches.

There is a contrast between Odysseus and the heroes in the *Iliad*, none of whom would likely have endured the kind of insults and abuses that Odysseus takes without a whimper from the suitors, nor would they have considered concealing their identity, even to further a noble goal such as the destruction of the suitors. However, the heroes of the *Iliad* were locked into an almost ritual pattern of behavior that is suited only to war and the battlefield. Odysseus has his place in that heroic environment as well, but in the *Odyssey*, Homer depicts what it means to be a hero off the battlefield as well as on it. Odysseus faces circumstances that are enormously different from those he has to contend with during the war, and he responds to them in an appropriately heroic fashion. Homer broadens the definition of a hero in these ways.

Human Condition

The question of what it means to be a human is an important theme in the *Odyssey*. The poem provides various examples of human beings: good, bad, young, old, acting along and acting in groups, living on earth and as spirits in the underworld. Each of these types is an integral part of the story of Odysseus and his effort to discover the essence of the human condition.

There are two incidents in the epic that highlight the importance of this theme for Homer. They are Odysseus's refusal of Calypso's offer to make him immortal (V.215-24), and Achilles's reply to Odysseus's attempt at consolation in the underworld when Achilles says that he would rather be a poor servant in life than to have rank among the dead. To be human and to be alive, Homer implies, is to matter, to be important. The dead in the underworld, like the gods on Olympus, may have a kind of existence, but it is ultimately an empty one.

Love and Loyalty

Love and loyalty are two important aspects of the human condition and also make an important theme in the *Odyssey*. The loyalty of Eumaeus, Eurycleia, and Philoetius, for example, stands in direct contrast to the behavior of Melantho, Melanthius, and the suitors, for which they are eventually punished. Helen and Menelaus are clearly in love, and there can be little doubt that Odysseus and Penelope feel much the same way, despite Odysseus's philandering on his way home and Penelope's testing of her husband when he finally reveals his true identity.

Love in the *Odyssey* is neither a tempestuous passion (as it sometimes seems to be in the *Iliad*, at least where Helen and Paris are concerned) nor a deathless romance as it would become in the lays of the Middle Ages. Love in the *Odyssey* is quieter and deeper. Odysseus and Penelope may not have a grand passion any longer, but the love they do have proves their relationship is secure; it is what pulls Odysseus home and what keeps Penelope hoping for his return.

Order and Disorder

From the very beginning of the poem, there are indications that there is supposed to be an order to life and those who ignore or threaten that order will be punished for it. The main component of that ordered system is *xenia*, the laws of hospitality. In a world without regular places for travelers to lodge and where neither police nor other international law-enforcement bodies exist, refusing shelter to a traveler or taking advantage of a guest under one's roof (or, as with the suitors, taking advantage of one's host) constitutes a serious breakdown in moral and civic order. Hence the laws of hospitality are raised to the level of a religious duty and to violate those laws merits the ultimate punishment.

But there are other indications of disorder in the poem as well. At the beginning of Book 2, for example, the assembly on Ithaca has not met since Odysseus left for Troy. This breakdown in civil order may have contributed to the suitors' ability to flout the laws of *xenia* for almost four years. Surely, if there had been any kind of regular functioning government in Odysseus's absence, it would have put an end to their degradations, and Odysseus would not have had to slaughter more than a hundred people on his return home. The implication seems clear that rules of social conduct matter in the Homeric world and that even small violations of those rules can have disastrous consequences.

Structure

In general, the *Odyssey* is more technically advanced than the *Iliad*. The flashbacks that seemed so awkward in the earlier poem are handled much more subtly; for example, the action jumps seamlessly from one place to another even in the middle of a book and is itself much more lively than the formalized battle scenes in the *Iliad*. The epic focuses on the return trip, so the use of flashbacks seems to underscore the role of memory in the characters' present experience. Those returning from war remember the battle scenes; those left behind remember the moments of departure; those waiting remember how long it has been since they were reunited with loved ones. Narrative in this epic is pegged, in this way, to the function of memory, to the way the narrator can recall and relive past experience in the act of relating it in the present.

Meter

English meter involves patterns of stressed and unstressed syllables. Greek meter, by contrast, involves patterns of long and short syllables where, as a general rule, two short syllables equal one long syllable. Greek poetry does not rhyme either, although it does make use of alliteration and assonance (repeated use of the same or similar consonant patterns and vowel patterns, respectively) in order to string words together.

The *Odyssey* is written in dactylic hexameters, which set the standard form for epic poetry; in fact, this particular meter is sometimes referred to as epic meter or epic hexameter. *Hexameter* means that per line there are six feet (a unit like a measure in a line of music); *dactylic* refers to the particular metrical pattern of each foot—in this case, the basic pattern is one long syllable followed by two shorts, although variations on that basic pattern are allowed. (Dactylic compares to waltz time in music.) The final foot in each line, for example, is almost always a spondee (two long syllables, instead of one long and two shorts). The meter is sometimes varied to suit the action being described, using more dactyls when describing subjects that move quickly (horses galloping, for example), and more spondees when describing subjects the move slowly or are sad.

Similes

The epic similes so common in the *Iliad* are used much more sparingly in the *Odyssey*, which makes them all the more striking when they do appear. The simile is a comparison of an unfamiliar subject and a familiar one. The unfamiliar subject is the called the tenor and the subject to which it is compared is the vehicle. The comparison is made explicit by the use of *like* or *as*. The epic simile then uses *so* to return to the tenor of the comparison. The simile is a literary device that slows the action and emphasizes a particular moment or feeling. At the beginning of Book 20, the following two similes are used to describe Odysseus as he plots the downfall of the scheming maids and the suitors, respectively:

> The heart inside him growled low with rage, as a bitch mounting over her weak, defenseless puppies growls, facing a stranger, bristling for a showdown—so he growled from his depths, hackles rising at their outrage. (XX.13-16, Fagles)

> But he himself kept tossing, turning, intent as a cook before some white-hot blazing fire who rolls his sizzling sausage back and forth, packed with fat and blood—keen to broil it quickly, tossing, turning it, this way, that way—so he cast about. (XX.24-26, Fagles)

Compare & Contrast

- **Late Bronze Age:** Piracy is well-established, and ship-building evolves as a means of transporting soldiers who intend to rob distant coastal communities.

  Iron Age: Naval forces are an important part of conducting warfare; however, the Phoenicians increasingly control trade in the Mediterranean Sea.

Today: According to the International Maritime Bureau, incidents of piracy worldwide in 2009 surpass four hundred.

- **Late Bronze Age:** My cenean pottery is refined and ornate. It depicts figures in local dress and soldiers armed for battle.

  Iron Age: Geometric design in pottery glaze work develops, some of which shows abstract human figures involved in mourning the dead.

  Today: Geometric-style vases from the eighth century BCE are displayed in many museums around the world, one of which is the National Archeological Museum in Athens.

- **Late Bronze Age:** Writing is known, although mainly in cumbersome, syllabic forms such as Egyptian hieroglyphics, the Mycenaean Linear A and B scripts, or the Hittite/Akkadian cuneiform. Literacy is probably restricted to the highest levels of the aristocracy and a professional class of scribes, bureaucrats, or diplomats.

Iron Age: Literacy in the Greek-speaking world begins to be rediscovered using a different alphabet, in which each letter represents a particular sound and not an entire syllable. Literacy is restricted to the upper classes and some professionals, such as rhapsodes (those who recite poetry) and some artists.

Today: The vast majority of people, approximately 82 percent, are at least able to read and write well enough to conduct their own business affairs. In developed countries, the literacy rate is as high as 98 percent; however, in some underdeveloped countries only 25 percent of the people can read and write.

- **Late Bronze Age:** Sacked cities are pillaged and destroyed, often burned to the ground, the victors assuming the city is erased from human history.

  Iron Age: Many cities are built on the ruins of earlier communities because their location is valuable for various reasons.

  Today: Archeological research finds evidence in layers as certain sites are unearthed. Archeologists have determined that between 3000 BCE and 500 CE, at least nine separate cities existed on the site of Troy.

These similes convey a sense of Odysseus's feeling at this moment. The first compares the hero's unknown feeling to the well-known growl of a female dog over her puppies; the second compares the way Odysseus refines his plan of attack to the well-known image of a cook moving sausage back and forth over a flame with his fork, preparing it for dinner. The hero's emotional state and the way his plan develops in his mind are conveyed through the known subjects to which they are compared.

The Bronze Age

The Trojan War and its aftermath took place around 1250 BCE, the date of the wealthy burials found by Heinrich Schliemann (1822–1890) in Grave Circle A at Mycenae in 1873. For this reason, the period is sometimes also called the Mycenaean era. This was a time of relative stability, though not, of course, without its conflicts, wars, and raids. The dominant powers in the eastern Mediterranean were the Hittites in the central part of what is now Turkey, the Egyptians in what is now called the Middle East, and the Mycenaean kings in Greece and the surrounding islands.

The Bronze Age is so named because sometime between about 3000 and 1200 BCE and at different times during this period in different locations, human cultures began combining copper with tin and arsenic to form the alloy bronze, a metal that was stronger than pure copper and reasonably easy to smelt and use to create tools, weapons, and other articles. Initially, copper was probably found on the surface in nuggets, but gradually people discovered that where many of these nuggets were found there was more of the material buried, and in this way, mining evolved.

Trade flourished, quite surprisingly given the uncertainties of shipping and other means of transportation, together with a relatively low level of technological advancement (at least when considered by modern standards). Distinctive Mycenaean pottery, whether as art pieces intended for display and ceremonial use or for transporting trade goods such as oil, grain, or perfume, is found all over the Mediterranean basin in large quantities throughout this period.

Modern archeologists have determined that the ancient city of Ilium (later called Troy) was sacked repeatedly. It was a rich, fortressed community, powerful because its location allowed it to control the southern approach to the Hellespont (Dardanelles). Neighboring and distant kingdoms envied its dominance and wanted to steal its riches. Thus, repeatedly, the ancient city was attacked, sacked, and burned. These conflicts continued for many years, and robbery, rather than reclaiming the abducted Helen was the motive.

The Iron Age

Beginning around the eleventh century BCE, the Greeks began to use iron in place of bronze, to cremate their dead as opposed to burying them intact, and to establish colonies along the west coast of what is now Turkey. By Homer's day, roughly the middle of the eighth century BCE, these trends were well-established.

Writing was rediscovered using a new alphabet borrowed from the Phoenicians, and foreign trade improved, helped in no small part by the colonies along the Ionian coast which, while typically independent of their mother cities, nevertheless tended to remain on friendly terms with them. The population was again on the rise, which spurred another wave of colonization, this time chiefly toward the west, to Sicily, parts of Italy, and the south of France.

At least on the Greek mainland, the era of kings rapidly drew to a close. By the beginning of the eighth century, the nobles had taken the reins of power from the kings almost everywhere and were ruling over family groups or tribes in what would come to be called the *polis*, or city-state.

Largely because of the decorations found on pottery from the period, this era has come to be known as the Geometric period, but increasing regularity was a feature of more than just the decorative arts. In this period the beginnings of Greek national identity emerge, prompting and/or prompted by the founding of the Olympic games and the dissemination of Homer's works, among other factors. There is also evidence that more coordinated military tactics were beginning to be used.

Religious practices, if not beliefs, also seem to have begun a process of standardization. While the Homeric heroes sometimes go to specific places for religious observances, the majority seem to be family-or group-centered rituals that take place wherever the family or group may happen to be at the moment of the ritual, and archaeological evidence from the Bronze Age tends to confirm this view. Formal altars, like the one at the fountain described in Book 17, are known from the Bronze Age, but temples, buildings specifically set aside for formal public worship, have not been identified in the archaeological record much before the ninth century BCE and become much more frequent thereafter.

After Homer's day, while the population, wealth, commerce, and industry of Greece were generally on the rise, the political pendulum swung back and forth from more aristocratic and democratic models to varying forms of one man rule until just before the dawn of the Golden Age in the fifth century BCE.

Critical Overview

The critical reputation of the *Odyssey* is perhaps best demonstrated by noting that it is generally regarded as one of the first works of true literature in Western culture. This is significant not only because the poem stands near the head of the list, as it were, but also because it had to beat out a fair amount of competition to achieve that status.

By the middle of the sixth century BCE, around the same time as the Peisistratids in Athens ordered the first standard edition of Homer's works to be made, there were at least six other epic poems treating various parts of the Trojan War story. Most of these were fairly short, but the *Cypria*, which covered everything from the decision of the gods to cause the war through Agamemnon's quarrel with Achilles that begins Homer's work, was at least half as long as the *Iliad*. Unlike the *Iliad* and the *Odyssey*, however, none of the other poems in this epic cycle has survived except in fragmentary quotations in the works of later authors.

Certainly by the beginning of the sixth century, and possibly late in the seventh, there was already a group of poet/performers calling themselves the *Homeridae* (meaning *Sons of Homer*). This group may have been the forerunner of the *rhapsodes*, trained singers who, while they did apparently compose and improvise works of their own, were best known for reciting Homer's poetry. At least on

Plato's authority, the rhapsodes seem to have begun taking liberties with the poems, which may have led the Peisistratids to have the official text written down for the judges at the Great Panathenaia (a religious festival in honor of Athena held every four years) that included a contest for the rhapsodes that required them, presumably in shifts and over several days, to recite the whole of the *Iliad* and the *Odyssey*.

For most people, those public performances were probably their major form of exposure to Homer's work. For the educated class, however, knowing one's Homer quickly became the sign of culture and refinement. Homer is mentioned by name at least six hundred times in surviving Greek literature, in works of history, philosophy, religion, and law. In his *Poetics*, Aristotle holds Homer up as the "supreme poet in the serious style" and the forerunner of both tragedy and comedy. Herodotus, in his *Histories*, even credits Homer, along with his near contemporary Hesiod, with being the one who gave Greek religion its standard forms: the names, spheres and functions, and descriptions and descent of the gods.

The one dissenting voice in the ancient world seems to have been that of Plato. Although he quotes Homer on more than one occasion, and even lampoons the rhapsodes and their beautification or embellishment of the standard text in his dialogue *Ion*, in the *Republic*, his lengthy discussion of the ideal state and the education of its leaders, Plato dismisses Homer as a mere imitator and excludes him (and poets generally) from his educational program.

Homer was frequently imitated in the classical world, whether by the authors of the other poems in the epic cycle or lampooned as he was by Aristophanes in several of his plays (especially *The Birds* and *The Clouds*), yet his work was never equaled. Roman literature in particular owes a great deal to Homer, and to the *Odyssey* in particular: Later authors dated the beginnings of their national literature to a translation of the *Odyssey* into Latin made by the slave Livius Andronicus around 220 BCE), and the great Roman national epic the *Aeneid* not only uses Homer's epic hexameter line, it consciously imitates themes and events from both the *Iliad* and the *Odyssey*.

Interest in Homer continued well into the Christian era, as seen by Macrobius's *Saturnalia* (dated to the early part of the fifth century CE), when educated Romans still knew their Greek and spent an evening discussing the relative merits of Homer's treatment of the Troy story in comparison to Virgil's. With the fall of Rome in 455 CE), however, Homer and his works fell into obscurity for roughly one thousand years, until Renaissance scholars rediscovered classical texts and learned to read Greek. According to Philip Ford in his article "Homer in the French Renaissance," although the name Homer was associated with the ideal of an inspired poet, it was not until Petrarch requested a translation and read Homer's two epics that interest was renewed in the works.

The story of Odysseus received somewhat less attention than did the story of the Trojan War, but it never entirely died out. The French moralist François de Fe´nelon turned the story of Telemachus into a Christian fable with his 1699 publication of *Les Aventures Télémaque*, and the Spanish poet Pedro Caldero´n did the same with the story of Odysseus and Circe.

Interest in Homer and his works was revived in the eighteenth century when F. A. Wolf first proposed the Homeric question, regarding who wrote what and when. Johann Wolfgang von Goethe started, but did not finish, a romantic tragedy about Odysseus and Nausicaa. It is thought that Milton was influenced by Homer in composing *Paradise Lost*, and Homer certainly inspired later poets such as Byron and Tennyson, though their works are narrower in scope. The plethora of resources on Homer in libraries and on the Internet confirms that his works are ever growing in their appeal. In fact, a 2007 collection of essays gathered by Barbara Graziosi and Emily Greenwood emphasizes the impact of Homer in the twentieth century, moving from an already revered position as the starting point of all great Western literature to that of a classic of all world literature. Obviously, the *Odyssey* continues to enjoy the critical acclaim and popular interest that have been associated with it throughout most of the two and a half millennia since it was first written.

Sources

Biers, William R., *The Archaeology of Greece: An Introduction*, Cornell University Press, 1996.

Butler, Samuel, *Authoress of the "Odyssey,"* 1897, reprint, Forgotten Books, 2008.

Fagles, Robert, trans., *Odyssey* (Penguin Classics), by Homer, edited with introduction by Bernard Knox, Penguin Classics, 2006.

Ford, Philip, "Homer in the French Renaissance," in *Renaissance Quarterly*, Vol. 59, No. 1, 2006.

Graziosi, Barbara, and Emily Greenwood, eds., *Homer in the Twentieth Century: Between World Literature and the Western Canon*, Oxford University Press, 2007.

Griffin, Jasper, *Homer: The "Odyssey": A Student Guide*, 2nd ed., Cambridge University Press, 2004.

Jones, Peter V., "Introduction," in *The Odyssey*, translated by E. V. Rie, 1946, reprint, Penguin Classics, 1991, p. xi.

Levi, Peter, *The Pelican History of Greek Literature*, Penguin, 1985.

Further Reading

Bloom, Harold, ed., *Homer's The "Odyssey,"* Chelsea House, 2007.

> This book is an updated collection of ten essays with diverse critical approaches to the *Odyssey*.

Nagy, Gregory, *Homer the Classic (Hellenic Studies)*, Center for Hellenic Studies, 2010.

> This study traces the reception of Homer's poetry from the fifth through the first century BCE Nagy explains Homer's literary influence on the centuries that immediately followed him and also how his epics were used by individuals and states to promote certain cultural and political agenda. Nagy's purpose is to show how Homer's poems became classics during the years of when Athens flourished.

Paipetis, S.A., *The Unknown Technology in Homer (History of Mechanism and Machine Science)*, Springer, 2010.

> This English translation of a book originally written in Greek is a study of the scientific and technological knowledge contained in Homer's epics, which indicates a highly

advanced civilization in the Mycenaean era.

Stark, Freya, *Ionia: A Quest*, Tauris Parke, 2010.

Modern-day Ionia, including inland from the western shore, in the area in which Homer is purported to have lived, is the focus of this new book.

Wachsmann, Shelley, *Seagoing Ships and Seamanship in the Bronze Age Levant*, Texas A&M University Press, 2008.

This book offers a comprehensive study of how early eastern Mediterranean cultures took to the sea. Included are Aegeans, Minoans, Mycenaeans, among others. Wachsmann describes ship construction, piracy, laws pertaining to the sea, and Bronze Age shipwrecks.

Suggested Search Terms

Odyssey

Homer

Homer AND epic

Homer AND poet

Odysseus AND Penelope

Odysseus AND Calypso

Greek epic

Odysseus

Odysseus AND Cyclops

Odysseus AND Ithaca